A Great Idea

YouTube®

by Adam Woog

NORWOOD HOUSE PRESS

Norwood House Press
P.O. Box 316598
Chicago, Illinois 60631

For information regarding Norwood House Press, please visit our Web site at:

www.norwoodhousepress.com or call 866-565-2900.

PHOTO CREDITS: Cover: AP Images/Tony Avelar; AFP/Getty Images, 34; AP Images/Andy Manis, 15; AP Images/AP Photo, 21; AP Images/AP Photo/YouTube.com, 40; AP Images/B.K. Bangesh, 22; AP Images/Cameron Bloch, 18; AP Images/Daman Dovarganes, 42; AP Images/Darrell Hoemann, 8 (right); AP Images/Jennifer Graylock, 38; AP Images/Liu Junfeng, 11; AP Images/Todd Feeback, 19; Chris Pizzello/Reuters/Landov, 31; © Chris Stewart/San Francisco Chronicle/Corbis, 8 (left); © David J. Green-Lifestyle Themes/Alamy, 5; Getty Images, 29, 36; Hervé Hughes/Hemis/Corbis, 12; © Phototake, Inc./Alamy, 10; Reuters/Hans Deryk/Landov, 27

DEDICATION
For Misha Berson, who first got me watching YouTube.

LIBRARY OF CONGRESS CATALOGING-IN-PUBLICATION DATA

Woog, Adam, 1953–
  YouTube / by Adam Woog.
    p. cm. — (A great idea)
  Summary: "Describes the invention and development of YouTube. Includes glossary, websites, and bibliography for further reading"—Provided by publisher.
  Includes bibliographical references and index.
  ISBN-13: 978-1-59953-198-4 (library edition : alk. paper)
  ISBN-10: 1-59953-198-4 (library edition : alk. paper)
  1. YouTube (Electronic resource)—Juvenile literature. 2. Internet videos—Juvenile literature. 3. Online social networks—Juvenile literature. 4. YouTube (Firm)—Juvenile literature. I. Title. II. Title: You Tube.
  TK5105.8868.Y68W66 2008
  006.7—dc22
                                                              2008010724

Manufactured in the United States of America.

Contents

Note: Words that are **bolded** in the text are defined in the glossary on page 44.

Chapter 1

A Bright Idea

Peter Oakley was an unlikely video star. The shy, retired Englishman was in his eighties in 2006. That year Oakley started making short videos about his life. In his videos he shared his experiences during World War II. Oakley made his videos available for anyone to see on the Internet. Suddenly he was a star in countries around the world.

People liked his easy way of telling a story. They found his tales of wartime interesting. They also liked seeing an older man who could use new technology. In a short time, millions of people had seen Oakley's videos.

What made him a star was YouTube, the world's biggest video-sharing Web site. On YouTube, Oakley had a nickname. He was known as "**geriatric**1927." He and YouTube were both pioneers of online video. Today, watching videos on the Internet is not unusual. People do it all

Millions of people surf the Internet daily to read news, contact friends, play games, and watch the latest YouTube videos.

mation and entertainment, and a fun way to communicate with others the same age. However, this is not why the Internet is called a "young" technology. Most people who use the Internet today did not start until the 1990s, so it is not very old.

For many years, communicating by computer could be slow and expensive. But as the speed of computers increased and the price dropped, almost anyone could "surf the 'Net" at home, at school, or at work. As people came to expect more from the Internet, it began delivering more. They could connect with each other using email. They could buy and sell things. They could

the time. But before YouTube, almost no one had done such a thing. And that is why, when YouTube came along, it was such an amazing new idea.

Before YouTube

Millions of young people use the Internet every day. It is a good way to find infor-

The Two Main Guys

YouTube was started by three people, but two of them, Chad Hurley and Steve Chen, are most closely associated with it. Chad Hurley was born in 1977 and grew up in Pennsylvania. In high school, he was interested in computers. But his main interest was art, so he earned a college degree in that. Just before graduation, Hurley had a job interview with PayPal, a company that was just starting. He was asked to create a logo (a visual symbol) for the new company. PayPal hired Hurley—and they liked his logo so much that the company still uses it.

Steve Chen was born on the island of Taiwan in 1978. When he was still young, his family moved to the United States. They settled near Chicago, Illinois. Chen was always interested in math and computer science. He studied those subjects in high school and at the Illinois Mathematics and Science Academy. Chen also attended the University of Illinois at Urbana-Champaign. However, he left early to work for PayPal.

discover new facts. They could share photographs. They could even build their own Web sites.

Some things were still difficult. For example, it took a lot of time and effort to send short videos from one computer to another. It was also hard to **post** them on a Web site.

Three Friends Have an Idea

Late in 2004, three young men started talking about this problem. The three, all in their twenties, were Chad Hurley, Steve Chen, and Jawed Karim. They had worked together at PayPal, a small but very successful company, almost since it began in 2000. The company was based in northern California, south of San Francisco. This area is called Silicon Valley. It is the home of many computer and Internet companies. Silicon is a material used in making memory chips for computers.

While helping this company grow, Hurley, Chen, and Karim learned a lot about how to run a successful online business. Also, each owned a small part of the company. When it was sold in 2002, they earned a lot of money. They left their jobs, but did not retire from business. Instead, they decided to work together and start a new Internet company.

In the Beginning

Where did the idea for YouTube come from? There are two versions of this story, but no one has ever said which is correct. According to one account, Chen and Hurley had dinner together one night with

The Third Guy

The media usually does not pay much attention to the third founder of YouTube, Jawed Karim, because he has not been as active in the company as the other two. Karim was born in Germany in 1979. His father is from Bangladesh, and both of his parents are scientists. The family moved to the United States in 1992, and Karim went to high school in Saint Paul, Minnesota. Like Chen, Karim went to the University of Illinois but they did not meet there. Also like Chen, Karim left college early to join PayPal. After Karim helped start YouTube, he decided to leave the company. He wanted to finish his education in computer science. However, he kept many shares of stock and remained an adviser to the company. Recently, he started an organization called Youniversity Ventures. It helps launch new business ideas.

The three founders of YouTube (left, Chad Hurley and Steve Chen; far right, Jawed Karim) were in their twenties when they started the popular video site.

friends. They made videos and took photos of themselves and then tried to send them to other friends over the Internet. They had no trouble emailing the photos, but they found that it was very hard to send the videos—even though

the photos and videos were both taken by **digital** cameras.

The other version is that all three men were at a party. They talked about two very different news events. One was a terrible **tsunami** in Southeast Asia in 2004. The surging water killed hundreds of thousands of people—many because they had never seen the power of a tsunami before. The other was a performance by singer Janet Jackson at the Super Bowl. During one song, Jackson had a very embarrassing moment. Chen, Karim, and Hurley talked about how hard it was to find video clips of these events on the Internet.

It does not really matter which version of the story is correct. However it happened, the three started talking about

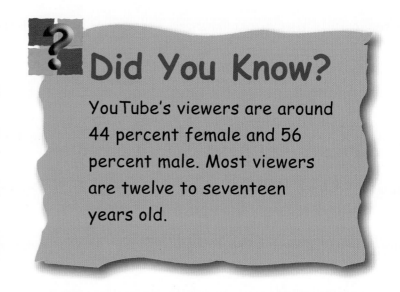

Did You Know?

YouTube's viewers are around 44 percent female and 56 percent male. Most viewers are twelve to seventeen years old.

finding and sharing short videos. They believed that there had to be an easier way to do this over the Internet. Furthermore, they thought they could figure out a way to do it.

This was not a new idea. Others had tried. A site called shareyourworld.com was probably the very first video-sharing Web site. It started in 1997, but soon went out of business. The technology of the time was just not good enough for sending and watching videos over the Internet.

By the early years of the twenty-first century, computers had become much more powerful. The fiber-optic lines that carried information around the planet were able to send larger files with much greater speed. Wireless technology, which moves information through the air, was also growing at a fast rate. For these reasons, Hurley, Chen, and Karim believed the timing was right for

The invention of fiber-optic lines (pictured) allowed larger files to be sent over the Internet.

Did You Know?

YouTube is the world's fastest growing Web site.

their idea. They set out to create a Web site that would serve as a central location, or **clearinghouse,** for videos. People would be able to post, or **upload,** short clips on this site. And anybody with a computer could go to the site to look at the clips that were posted.

A Virtual Village

First, Hurley, Karim, and Chen had to decide what kind of clips would be posted on their site. They also needed to decide how the clips might be used. They came up with several ideas. They considered building a site that would let people use video clips to sell things at online auctions. They also thought about creating a video dating service. People who used the service would post videos of them-selves. They also thought about a site that would be just for travel videos.

None of these ideas sounded very inter-esting. Finally, they asked themselves: *Why*

People from all over the world can post on YouTube, creating a global virtual village.

The founders of YouTube thought that skateboarders, for example, might enjoy watching videos of other skateboarders.

YouTube's Ancestors

YouTube is, in some ways, an Internet version of two popular TV shows. One of its creators, Chad Hurley, mentioned this when he told a reporter, "We are providing a stage where everyone can participate and everyone can be seen. . . . We see ourselves as a combination of *America's Funniest Home Videos* and *Entertainment Tonight.*"

does our site have to be one thing? Why can't it have a little of everything? They decided to let the people who visited their site decide what to post. They would just make it easy and fun. The more Hurley, Karim, and Chen talked, the better this

new idea sounded. It would be a **virtual** village!

They pictured people from all over the world—people who had the same interest or passion—coming to their site to share videos. The Internet was already full of words and pictures that explained how to do almost anything. A video Web site could bring these ideas to life! For example, people who loved to work in the garden could watch other gardeners in action. People who loved to skateboard could watch other skateboarders.

Creating such a site sounded like hard work. But it also sounded like fun. So the three made an office in Hurley's garage in the town of Menlo Park, California, and they went to work.

Chapter 2

Making Things Happen

Hurley, Chen, and Karim were smart and organized. In order to get the site started quickly, they divided their work based on strengths. Hurley's specialty was graphics, so he designed the **interface** and logo. That is, he worked on how the site would look and "feel" to a user. Chen and Karim, the computer experts, shared the technical problems. They started early in 2005.

Many decisions were made during the planning stages. For example, they wanted to keep things simple and easy to use. They were not designing a site for computer experts. They wanted to attract people with all levels of computer skills. So they chose software that was easy to use and free. This fit in well with their plans for the site. They did not want to restrict it only to people who could afford expensive software.

Serious and Silly

Some YouTube videos are very serious. For example, a California woman named Holly Schnaars had a serious form of cancer. She made YouTube clips to educate people about how to spot the disease.

Other clips are just for fun. For example, two young comedians, Matt Sloan and Aaron Yonda, created a series of low-budget comedy films making fun of *Star Wars*. These videos are about Chad Vader, Darth Vader's brother, who manages a grocery store. They became big hits. Matt and Aaron became two of YouTube's biggest stars, and their popularity led to other opportunities for them.

Filmmakers Aaron Yonda, in costume, and Matt Sloan, far right, prep for a new Chad Vader episode to be filmed in the office of Mayor Dave Cieslewicz, center, of Madison, Wisconsin.

These two decisions proved to be very important. Chen, Hurley, and Karim did not realize it at the time, but their new Web site would soon attract tens of millions of young people who loved to watch videos, but did not have much computer know-how or money.

YouTube 101

YouTube has become such a part of society that it has even inspired a university class. In 2007, Pitzer College in California offered a course called "Learning from YouTube." The teacher wanted students to think about YouTube's place in society. Her students looked at YouTube, posted comments, made their own videos, and met to talk about it.

Finally, they chose a name—YouTube—and a motto. Their motto was "Broadcast Yourself." Both the name and motto were symbols of their hope to let anyone and everyone freely use the site.

Show Time!

As their plan developed, Karim, Hurley, and Chen realized the Web site would need lots of **bandwidth** and storage space. Huge amounts of information had to flow in and out of the site, and every video uploaded by users needed to be stored somewhere. Getting this was going to be expensive. They had money of their own, but it was going to cost far more than they had. So they found a company that invests money in promising new businesses. This company invested millions of dollars in

YouTube. If the site was a success, the company would make back many times its investment.

By May 2005, YouTube had a test version of the site to show the public. Compared to what visitors see on YouTube today, the first clips were very simple. One clip showed Chen's cat playing. Another showed Karim standing in front of the elephant exhibit at the zoo. Another just showed the three YouTube creators hanging out and having fun in their garage office.

YouTube officially debuted in the later part of 2005. To build interest, the site held a contest. It gave away an iPod Nano every day for two months. People earned points by signing up, inviting others to do the same, or by posting a video. The more points people earned, the greater their chances of winning. Many curious Web surfers took a look.

Did You Know?

A number of people have become mainstream stars after becoming popular on YouTube. The first was probably Brooke Brodack. She was a receptionist in Connecticut who hoped to become a comedian. Her popularity on YouTube (performing as "Brookers") led to a contract with late-night TV host Carson Daly and other opportunities.

A woman views videos on the YouTube site. The clips are surrounded by information.

How It Works

The basics of how YouTube worked then and now are simple. The site has always been free. It makes its money by selling advertising space on the screen. Visitors can choose from the clips highlighted on the home page, or find videos by typing a few words into a search box. They do not have to sign up or sign in, and can watch as many clips as they like.

Each video is shown in a small box, surrounded by information that includes how many times it has been viewed and how many stars (1 to 5) it has been given by other people. Videos can be enlarged to fit the entire screen. They also can be emailed to a friend. Some visitors choose to become registered users. Only registered users are allowed to post videos. Videos for YouTube can be created by a digital camera, cell phone or webcam. Registered users can also create "channels" of related videos, save videos, post comments, and make **playlists**. They can even subscribe to other people's channels to automatically learn about new videos. Registered users sometimes insert YouTube videos into other **file-sharing** Web sites. They can also restrict videos so that only certain viewers can watch them.

More Features

Another feature for registered users is TestTube. This is where YouTube tests new ideas. With it, users can help shape the site's future. For example, one idea that people tested was a feature called Streams. It let people chat

Registered users of YouTube can post their own homemade videos.

with other members who were viewing the same video. If ideas tried out on Test-Tube prove to be popular, they might become part of YouTube's regular features.

Some people choose to open a Director's Account. This is mainly for amateur filmmakers. It has several advantages. For example, directors can post videos that are longer than YouTube's ten-minute limit. Also, they can link videos to their personal Web sites.

YouTube also has a "Featured Videos" section. This changes all the time. Viewers vote on their favorites and the YouTube staff highlights the best.

Copyright Problems

As it has evolved, YouTube experienced a number of problems. One of the most serious involved videos that were posted without permission from their creators. A clip called "Lazy Sunday" is an example of this. "Lazy Sunday" is a short film that was originally shown on TV's *Saturday Night Live* in December 2005. Someone recorded the video and posted it on YouTube, where it became wildly popular. Many people who had missed the TV show heard they could see "Lazy Sunday" on YouTube. This drew millions of new viewers to the site.

The network that owned *Saturday Night Live* was pleased that so many people wanted to see the video, but it had not given YouTube permission to show the film. The network believed that YouTube had violated copyright law by showing something it did not own. A copyright law protects something that has been created, such as a movie, TV show, book, or song. The network could have asked that YouTube be punished—even though someone else had posted the video—because YouTube had created the place where this copyrighted work had been shown.

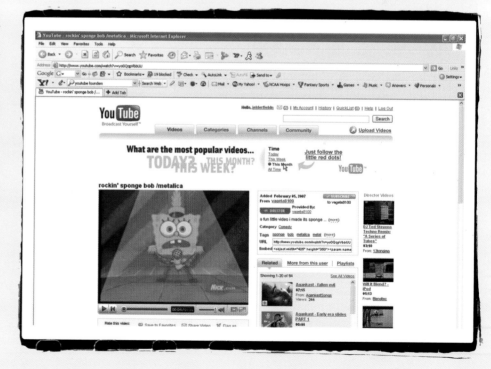

Nickelodeon, the company that owns SpongeBob SquarePants, sued YouTube for posting the character's image without permission.

Despite numerous competing video Web sites YouTube remains the most popular video-sharing site. A viewer opens up a YouTube video.

YouTube has tried to be careful about respecting the copyrights of others. For example, early on, some people posted entire movies. YouTube responded to this problem by limiting the length of clips, in most cases, to ten minutes.

More Challenges

Another problem faced by YouTube is material that might offend some people. The site tries to restrict some clips to adult viewers only. And it completely bans clips that have violence or are inappropriate in other ways. To do this, YouTube uses **censors**. These people watch the videos once they are posted to make sure they do not break the rules. However, so many clips are posted that not all can be checked. Some videos that do not belong on YouTube manage to slip through. So YouTube relies on the users themselves to report problems. This is similar to the "community policing" used by other public Web sites. It works fairly well.

Another challenge YouTube faces is competition. As YouTube's popularity took off, so did the idea of video-sharing sites. Within a year, YouTube had competitors. However, YouTube continued to be the biggest and most popular of these sites. Some sources say that YouTube gets 70 million visits a day. *PC World* magazine reported that almost 43 percent of all visits to video Web sites during one week in May 2006 were to YouTube. The second-most visited site had about half as many visits. By the summer of 2006, YouTube was one of the fastest-growing and most visited sites of any kind on the Internet.

YouTube Communities

YouTube's loyal fans number in the millions. Within this big group are countless smaller ones. These smaller groups form "communities" that gather over the Internet. Members view and discuss videos that interest them, and share their ideas with others who have done the same.

In this way, YouTube has changed the way the world communicates. It has made it easier for people to share ideas and in-terests no matter who they are or where they live.

Did You Know?

The YouTube member with the most channel subscribers, as of April 20, 2008, is Smoosh. Smoosh is a rock band built around two young sisters from Seattle, Washington, who go only by their first names: Chloe and Asya.

Chapter 3

Changing the World

YouTube is now one of many video-sharing sites on the Internet. However, YouTube is still by far the most popular. As of early 2008, only a few years after it officially started, YouTube boasted more than half a million registered users. It also had millions of casual guests—people who just visit every once in a while.

All of these people are watching—*a lot*. Every day, about 100 million videos are viewed on YouTube. And the site is growing at an amazing pace. About seventy thousand clips are added every day. That means that more than two hundred hours of new video are being added every hour of every day!

Though YouTube was created in the United States, its audience spans the globe. This was one of the original goals of Chen, Hurley, and Karim. By the summer of 2007, YouTube was available in French,

Spanish, Portuguese, Italian, Japanese, Polish, and Dutch.

That's one of the great things about YouTube—it has something for everyone, regardless of their age, nationality, or interests.

Kid Stuff

When YouTube's three inventors were designing their Web site, they probably did not realize how important it would become to young people. Today, boys and girls between the ages of twelve and seventeen make up the largest group of YouTube viewers. In fact, there are more users in this age range than all other ages combined.

What is it that young Web surfers like so much about YouTube? Above all else, they like that YouTube offers so many ways to connect with people they know, and people they don't. Many kids say they dream up unusual ideas, type a few key words into the search window, and see if someone else has thought of the same weird concept and actually made a

YouTube Is Global

Sometimes, YouTube fans meet in person. For example, "YouTubers" sometimes get together for conventions. At these meetings, people can meet (and film) each other and their favorite YouTube celebrities.

Most of the time, however, these people do not meet in person. Instead, the Internet links people into virtual communities that "meet" at the same time all over the world.

video. They also like the rating system for videos—it feels good to know your vote counts as much as an adult's.

Young YouTube visitors also like to email their favorite videos to friends and classmates. If a video gets "hot" it gives everyone something to talk about at school. And when kids make a video and upload it to YouTube, everyone in class is sure to hear about it!

The Presidential Election

For older users, YouTube has become an important political force. For example, the site played a part in the **primaries**

CNN collected questions from YouTube viewers to use in their airing of the 2008 primary debates.

leading to the 2008 U.S. presidential election. During the primaries, the cable news channel CNN aired two **debates** between candidates, one for the Democratic Party and one for the Republicans.

Such debates are not unusual. What was different this time was how questions for the candidates were gathered. Debate questions often come from reporters or people picked by the candidates from the audience. For these debates, the questions came from YouTube users. They sent their questions to CNN ahead of time. CNN decided which questions to ask the candidates. The debates were very popular. For instance, the one with the Democratic candidates was seen by about 2.6 million viewers. That made it the second-most watched debate of 2007.

YouTube had an impact on the 2008 presidential campaign in other ways. Flyers and TV ads used to be the most common ways for candidates to get their message to voters. But several candidates in this election saw a way to reach even more people. They posted campaign videos on YouTube. Most of these were serious, such as Republican John McCain commenting on his feelings about the Iraq war. However, some were light-hearted, such as a funny spot for Hillary Clinton showing comedian and **activist** Rob Reiner giving advice to Clinton volunteers.

What's On?

The presidential debates are one example of YouTube's important place in American life. YouTube has touched people in other ways too. People who want to tell the world about—or hear about—serious and sometimes tragic news events are connecting with other people on YouTube.

One such event was Hurricane Katrina, which hit the U.S. Gulf Coast in 2005. People in New Orleans, Louisiana, and other hard-hit areas posted their eyewitness accounts of the destruction that occurred on YouTube. Many other examples include videos from people on both sides of the conflict in Iraq, or videos concerning political demonstrations in Tibet in the spring of 2008.

In this way, YouTube has given people a new way to communicate about important events. They do not have to wait for the news

YouTube users in New Orleans, Louisiana, posted videos of the devastation from Hurricane Katrina that occurred in their neighborhoods.

media to take notice of a story. They can grab a video camera and tell the story themselves.

Widening the Spotlight

YouTube has also changed the way performers reach their audiences. At one time, musicians and actors who were just starting out played in front of small crowds. They performed in tiny clubs and theaters, hoping their fans would spread the word. A few lucky ones were "discovered" by companies that backed them, and they became famous. Most never made it. Thanks to YouTube, a talented artist can be seen by millions of people. A few have even become stars on the YouTube Web site.

For example, in 2006 the Los Angeles–based band OK Go made a video for the song "Here It Goes Again." The tune is also called "The Treadmill Song," because the video shows the band moving around in step on a set of treadmills while

Blocking YouTube

YouTube reaches around the world, but not every place welcomes it. For instance, the site is partly or completely blocked in countries such as Morocco, Turkey, and the United Arab Emirates. This is mainly because some religious members in those countries do not approve of it. Also, some schools in the United States ban or filter YouTube. One reason is that they do not want to encourage students to post videos of bullying or fighting.

Members of the band OK Go won a Grammy for a video that they posted on YouTube. The band was relatively unknown before YouTube users made the video a hit.

In May 2008, police in Los Angeles arrested a man because police saw YouTube videos that showed him painting graffiti. Cyrus Yazdani was an artist and convention planner. But as "Buket" he also "tagged" hundreds of walls, signs, overpasses, and buses. Yazdani posted many of his adventures in vandalism on YouTube, complete with rap soundtracks. These helped the police find and arrest him.

singing. When the band uploaded this video on YouTube, it got more than 28 million hits. The clever video was a huge boost to the band's career. It won the band a **Grammy** Award in 2007.

YouTube has more in store for the world's musicians and music lovers. It is building a huge library of music videos. This would help musicians by exposing them to many viewers. Although music videos are aired on cable TV networks, YouTube enables users to choose what they watch, or explore the choices other users have made.

This is very exciting for the music business, and also for YouTube. Steve Chen told reporters in 2006 that he hoped that within a year and a half the site would "have every music video ever created."

Amateur Ad Makes Good

Sometimes posting a video for fun on YouTube can have very unusual and unexpected results. For example, in 2007 a British fan of Apple products, Nick Haley, posted a homemade commercial about the then-new iPod Touch on YouTube. Executives at Apple's headquarters in Cupertino, California, saw the ad.

But they did not get angry and tell him to stop. Just the opposite! They bought his ad. They flew Haley, a teenage student at the University of Leeds, to Los Angeles. They gave him money to reshoot the ad in high definition. Then they broadcasted it on national television during that year's World Series.

Pros and Amateurs

Not long ago, video cameras recorded images on tape. When the tapes were full, they were stored in boxes to be played again. Making scenes from those tapes into a short video clip—and getting that clip onto a computer—took great expertise. Today, video cameras record digitally. That means words and pictures can be **downloaded** directly onto a computer. From there, clips can be edited and uploaded to sites like YouTube with just a little practice.

Every day, amateur videos look more and more like they were made by professionals. A close look at some YouTube videos also shows that many that are made by "pros" have an "amateur" look that so many people love. That is one of the big influences YouTube has had on modern culture.

People who know how to make movies, as well as people who do not, can become

YouTube stars. It does not matter if the maker is a professional. A video just has to catch the public's eye. And this can happen with any video—whether serious or silly.

You!

In 2006 *Time* magazine named YouTube "Best Invention of the Year." That same year, as it does every year, *Time* also announced its "Person of the Year" award. This award is given to people who make a major impact on world events. In 2004, for

Time magazine highlighted YouTube's influence on the world when it gave "You" its "Person of the Year" award in 2006.

example, it was given to President George W. Bush. And in 2005 Bill and Melinda Gates and the singer Bono received it. In 2006, *Time's* award went to "You." The cover for *Time* that week showed a YouTube screen with a foil mirror—a reflection of the person looking into it.

The magazine singled out YouTube, along with the online encyclopedia *Wikipedia* and the online social network MySpace. It said that these three sites are changing the world. People all over the globe can connect with each other far more easily than ever before. And they no longer have to rely on "big business" for information and entertainment.

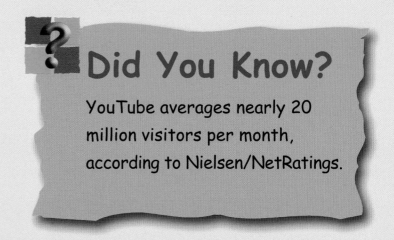

Did You Know?

YouTube averages nearly 20 million visitors per month, according to Nielsen/NetRatings.

Chapter 4

What's Next?

In the summer of 2007, the rap music star and actor Sean Combs—better known as Diddy—needed a new assistant. He did not place an ad in a newspaper. Nor did he ask his friends for suggestions. Instead, Diddy created an unusual help wanted video and posted it on YouTube. He

Rap music star Diddy used YouTube to advertise for an assistant position and received over 10,000 replies.

asked people to upload their own short videos on the site in reply. He wanted people to say in these responses why they thought they should be chosen as his new assistant.

In his video, Diddy seemed excited and pleased about using YouTube in this way. He hoped that it would put people at ease. He said, "It's a new age, new time, new era. Forget coming into the office and having a meeting with me and being all nervous."

Diddy was overwhelmed with the number of responses. An estimated ten thousand people sent in videos to YouTube. In fact, so many people replied that Diddy had to post a second notice, saying that only college graduates could apply for the job. He added that he would let YouTube viewers pick the finalists, but he would choose the final winner. He said that he hoped to do this on a reality TV show.

Helping Communities

Diddy's search for an assistant is just one example of the many new directions that video sharing on the Internet might take in the future. For example, one of these directions is being tried by nonprofit groups that help communities.

These groups use video-sharing sites like YouTube to raise money for good causes, or to make the public aware of important topics. By "advertising" on YouTube, they can reach thousands, even millions of people quickly and cheaply. Furthermore, these groups can spread the word about important topics by themselves. They do not have to wait for a newspaper or television reporter to tell their story.

For example, a church in Brooklyn, New York, had a beautiful organ that needed repair. The members of the church could not afford to fix it. However, they raised enough money for the project by making videos for YouTube. With just two videos, thousands of dollars came in from all around the world.

On a larger scale British rock star Peter Gabriel started an organization called Witness.org. It helps people use video to tell the world about **human rights abuses**. Witness.org provides people (many of them very poor) with video equipment and training. The organization also helps

British rock star Peter Gabriel uses YouTube to promote the videos produced by filmmakers for his organization Witness.org. The group provides video equipment to filmmakers around the world to document human rights abuses.

these people get their message out. It brings attention to people in need or in danger, such as the victims of land mines in the African country of Senegal.

Innovative Uses

A related idea to Witness.org comes from a company that sells video cameras that make uploading to the Internet quick and simple. This company hopes to give away a million of these cameras to nonprofit groups. It will then help the groups post their work online. The idea is to let people record events that traditional media might ignore. These events could be anything from breaking news in remote areas to little-known and rarely seen cultural events.

Some commercial businesses are also finding new uses for Internet video shar-

ing. For example, real estate agents help people buy or sell houses. Some real estate agents have started posting videos of homes for sale. These videos take buyers on "house tours" when they are hundreds or thousands of miles away.

Government organizations have started to use the power of shared video too. They use it to broadcast such things as public service announcements. For example, in 2006 the Office of National Drug Control Policy (ONDCP) became the first

government agency to run antidrug messages on YouTube.

New Styles

Other changes in the future will depend on developments in technology. Back in 2005, YouTube became possible because of breakthroughs in the Internet and computing power. This new technology allowed YouTube's creators to overcome earlier problems that had prevented video sharing from having success.

Since then, YouTube has made it easier for many other video-sharing sites. All of them are competing with YouTube. Some will make it. Some will not. And new ones will launch every year. All of them hope to be better, faster, easier, or more interesting than YouTube, the pioneer.

YouTube will try to stay ahead of the competition by looking for ways to use new technology, and by finding partners that help them reach people in new ways. For example, in 2008 YouTube was available on many mobile devices, such as cellular phones. This made it more convenient for people to visit YouTube, and also made it easier to sell phones to YouTube users.

Google and YouTube

YouTube's most important partner is the search engine called Google. Google bought YouTube in 2007. One of the first things Google did was experiment with adding YouTube clips to Google Earth. Google Earth is a feature that shows satellite photos of nearly every spot on earth.

Future Filmmakers

As video-sharing sites become more popular, they will probably start to sponsor events that now are typically done through other media. For example, they will probably sponsor film festivals. One short-film contest, for original videos two to seven minutes long, has already been held on YouTube. It was called Project Direct. The grand prize winner in this contest was a Brazilian film, *Laços* (*Ties*). It was about a young woman who meets a surprising stranger after leaving her father's funeral.

Google started working on software that lets people add their own videos to these photos. For example, someone looking at a satellite photo of the Eiffel Tower in Paris, France, could also see video clips that YouTube users have taken there.

Another piece of new technology that is likely to become popular is P2P (peer-to-peer) video. Peer-to-peer refers to connections among individuals. P2P video will let people swap clips directly, without having to go to a site like YouTube in between. Already, several companies are exploring this technology.

Meanwhile, several hardware companies that make cameras and other gadgets are working on new technology. They are developing features specifically designed for video-sharing sites. Among the products they are working on are cameras that will let people post clips directly to the Internet, without first having to save them to a computer.

The Unknown

People have many ideas about what direction video-sharing sites will take in the future. However, no one knows exactly

Mac Padilla, 21, organizes his music files on his laptop using peer to peer (P2P) technology before downloading them to a personal music player.

what will happen. This part of the Internet will certainly change—but it will change in unexpected ways.

In the mid-1950s a new invention called television revolutionized how people communicated and looked at things. Decades later, video technology and cable networks created still more huge new changes. And a few decades after that, YouTube led yet another revolution—this time on the Internet.

But the end of the story is not yet known. Imagine yourself in the year 2080, sharing all the wondrous things you have experienced in your lifetime. What will YouTube look like then? In what

Fame

Artist Andy Warhol once said that in the future, everyone will be famous for fifteen minutes. Some observers have commented that YouTube and similar sites have brought that future a little closer. Now anyone can become a video star. Journalist Erik Lacitis writes, "It's not so hard getting 15 minutes of fame, especially in these YouTube times where all it takes is a little luck and the right gimmick."

other ways will people exchange images and ideas? The answers to these questions are uncertain, but in the meantime, people can just sit back and enjoy the show that YouTube started.

Glossary

activist: Someone who works to advance a particular cause.

bandwidth: The amount of information that can be carried on a communications system, such as a cable or modem.

censor: Someone who checks movies, music, books, or magazines to make sure they do not contain anything offensive or illegal.

clearinghouse: A central place where material can be collected.

debate: A formal argument or discussion held in public.

digital: The term used to describe information that is stored electronically, in series of ones and zeroes. Computers use digital technology.

download: To transfer information (such as a video) from one computer or Web site to another.

file sharing: To share information (such as a video) with someone else via computer.

human rights abuses: Violations of basic rights such as freedom.

interface: The point where two different things, such as a computer and a person, connect.

geriatric: Elderly.

Grammy: An award given for out-standing achievement in the music industry.

playlists: Lists of favorite songs or videos, stored so that they can be watched or listened to at any time.

post: To transfer information (such as a video) from your computer to another computer or Web site.

primaries: Elections held to determine candidates from a field of many possible candidates.

tsunami: A very large ocean wave caused by an underwater earthquake or volcanic eruption.

upload: To transfer information (such as a video) from your computer to another computer or Web site.

virtual: Occurring or existing primarily online.

Books

Duffield, Katy. *YouTube: Chad Hurley, Steve Chen, Jawed Karim.* Detroit, MI: Kidhaven Press, 2008.

Miller, Michael. *YouTube 4 You.* Indianapolis, IN: Que Education, 2007.

On the Web

KidVideos.com: Videos for Kids, by Kids (http://kidvideos.com). This is a safe site that lets kids post, watch, and send videos to friends.

ME:TV! (www.nick.com/metv). This site, created by Nickelodeon, is another video-sharing site for kids. It emphasizes Nickelodeon and its shows.

YouTube: Broadcast Yourself (www.youtube.com). This is the source for the biggest and most popular of the Internet's video-sharing sites.

Index

 About the Author

Adam Woog has written many books for adults, young readers, and children. He has a special interest in history, biography, music, and the movies. Woog lives with his wife and daughter in Seattle, Washington.